Introduction:

You need to know a little about my horse's past to fully appreciate and understand Neville's story. I didn't want this book to be about the hardships that Neville has had to face before he came to live with us, but more about the journey that he and I have been on during our time together. Unfortunately you cannot fully appreciate the magic of this horse and the trust he has now placed in me, without a little knowledge of his past.

No place names or people's identities will be included. Those of you who may recognise some parts of the early years of his life, I hope it is you that cared for him in his hours of true need. I cannot for the life of me ever imagine the individuals who put Neville through his horror years, would be the type to choose to read his story. Neville is a pedigreed Arabian horse, very well bred, now beautiful, and as in most Arabians, full of life. When he came to us, he was an angry, untrusting individual, and incredibly head shy.

For a young horse, just 7 years old, I was his 5th owner. He'd been nowhere long enough to be taught true all round good manners, and his go-to attitude was self defence. My childhood dream like most young horse loving girls was to own a beautiful Arab and to have him at home, my dream came true in my 59th year.

I found him on a well-known website, he was advertised as a 7 year old Arab gelding, good to hack out alone or in company & good to have feet trimmed. I was looking for a 14 - 14.2hh Arab gelding, Neville almost fitted the bill. Plans were made to go and view him. It was a 4 hour journey, and to not waste the current owners time, I advised them it was a couple of months too soon, but we'd be more than happy to cover all costs if they could hold him until we had everything ready here at home.

It was then I was told in more detail that this horse had been found half starved in a field with very little grazing, limited water, standing guard over the corpse of his only companion. Upon investigating it appeared the other horse had been dead a couple of weeks. I dread to think what Neville had been feeling in that field, alone, scared, half starved, covered in scars from untreated injuries and worm laden. He was found, rescued & went to a further 2 homes before coming to me. I decided pretty much before viewing him that no matter what he was like, he'd have a forever home with us, hopefully ridden, pampered and cared for.

I had already committed myself to a half broken 15.1hh Arab gelding with more attitude than I'd ever bargained for.

That was our beginning together, I like to think the beginning of his true life which begun at 7.5 years of age when he was off loaded into our little yard by the professional haulier after a 4.5 hour journey. He came down the ramp with rivers of sweat running down his chest, legs and neck. He stunk of sweat and fear, and looked a broken horse, he aimed a half hearted hind leg at our little Whippet who was used to horses but not the type that kick!.... I wondered what on earth I'd seen in the rangy grey Arab gelding 6 weeks previous.

The story is just beginning

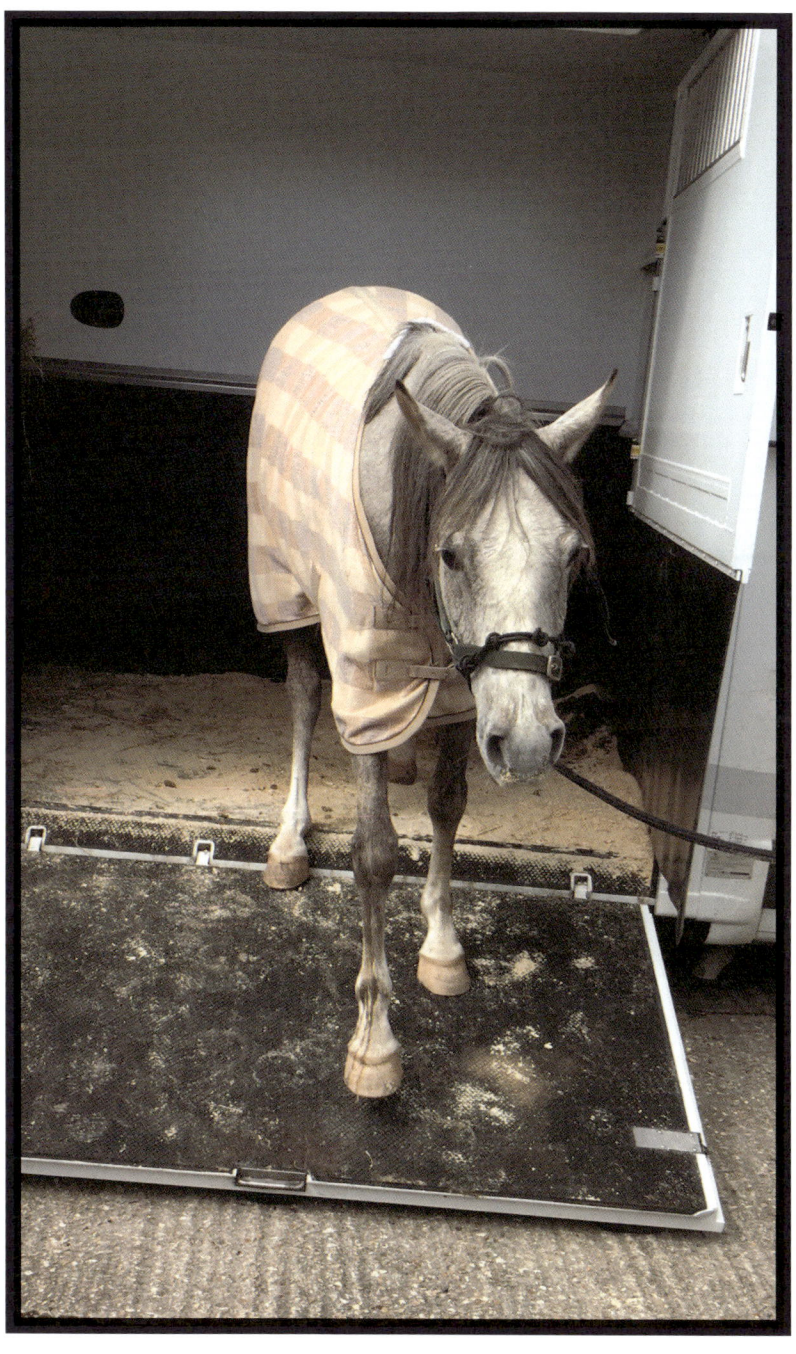

'Neville on the day he arrived dripping in sweat'

Chapter 1
Settling in

It wasn't long before I realised nothing was going to be simple dealing with a horse like Neville. It took me approximately an hour to coax Neville into his new stable, I wanted him to become fully adjusted to his new surroundings before it got dark that evening. It is a large stable but with a standard size doorway, which seemed to give him concern. It was just one of many things to cause Neville major anxieties I was soon to realise.

Simple things like changing rugs couldn't be done in a hurry, if I moved too quickly he would scoop his backend up and under himself and move out of my way. He was quite handy with his back feet and wouldn't hesitate to lift one up to threaten, but I have to say, in the three years of owning him he has never once connected his hoof to me. Neville's worst fault is his habit of biting, he can nip in frustration, he can nip for attention, he can nip if excited, and he can truly try and bite in temper!

Over the course of the next few months we settled into a rather pleasant routine, I changed my working hours the moment Neville came home, from full-time to working three days a week. This gave me two full days to dedicate to Neville as well as two weekend days to spend with Rod, sharing our time between Neville, Wilma our Whippet & Blossom our young cat. I found a wonderful foot trimmer called Deborah for Neville, and she has been a source of knowledge and is always there to help and advise. It was she that told me on her very first visit that Neville's diet needed fully adjusting and also the fact that there is an immense difference between a horse that does not wear shoes to a barefoot horse! 3 years on and we are nearly there in getting Neville's feet to be an even size and shape on all 4 feet. She's incredibly methodical & is always patient with my never ending questions regarding Neville's feet & overall well being. I truly believe a good Footrimmer knows far more than just feet. Not only does Neville really trust her she has become a family friend.

Having a horse in your life means that there are professionals that you have in your team on a regular basis, Neville's Footrimmer, Vet and saddle lady have all become friends and regular visitors. I was recommended to Sue, the lady who fits saddles, bridles and bits, and on her first visit I was amazed at her patience as Neville was far from easy to have his back measured and a variety of saddles placed on him. She advised that his current saddle that he come with wasn't ideal for him, and she had no saddle that would fit him, so a saddle was ordered to be made especially for Neville. My vet Antonia, bless her, has become my friend, lunch buddy and on those rare occasions when we both have the time, been my hacking buddy.

The true star member of the team is my husband Rod, who has the patience of a saint, and without him, having Neville at home would never have been possible. Rod is the most hard-working person I know and he never fails to surprise me with the ideas that he comes up with. Together we converted one of the old outbuildings into the most beautiful stable with tackroom as well as feed room all under the same roof.

'Neville's 1st star luxury hotel'

We fenced off the 4 acre field into smaller paddocks to ensure Neville had grazing all year round, and started the bare bones of a round pen. We were to work on this roundpen for months. It was a true labour of love, no machinery other than our trusty quad bike, trailer, shovels, rakes, wheelbarrows and plenty of blood, sweat and tears, but the finished result was awesome, and something I'm eternally grateful to Rod for all the hard physical graft he put into it.

We make a fantastic team and never have a cross word on these amazing projects. Rod always says to me that if I come up with the plan, he'll try and make it happen.

We're not 'well-off' and we work hard for what we buy, so paying for tradespeople is a no-go, if we want something made it's all down to us.

In his previous home Neville had other horses for company, but the owners had noticed Neville was a loner, he was at times ostracised from the other horses who most probably found Neville's high energy and yo-yo character was simply too much for their placid temperaments and they chose to ignore him. He would stand alone for most of the time where he was turned out day and night.

'Our fantastic roundpen has proved invaluable'

Here with us it didn't take long for Rod and I to realise our cat Blossom had chosen Neville as her new companion to terrorise at any opportunity she had! She is quite simply hysterical with the way she tends to dominate us all. She will choose to sit in the doorway of Neville's stable refusing to move and Neville quite amazingly who will have no qualms in walking straight over most humans, will never dream of standing up to Blossom. We have watched him stand in an open doorway for ages waiting for Blossom to move out of his way to enable him to walk out into his field. She will spend a lot of her time laying in the tackroom on the bed that I've put in there for her, just wiling away the hours if Neville is in there too. Rod even cut a catflap size hole in Neville's stable door to enable Blossom in the winter months when Neville's stable door is closed at night, to still go in and spend time with Neville if she wishes.

Out in the fields she will sit under him, she'll lay beside him, she'll also sit behind him playing with his tail in the breeze. Blossom is given the most freedom of our pets, but as a typical cat, has the attitude that she was born to be served. Sometimes we are honoured with her company on our bed at night, but other times who really knows where she is!

I was riding Neville three days a week with one evening ride. It was a wonderful opportunity to ride around our lanes seeing things in a completely different perspective than from inside a car. Neville being a high-spirited Dapple grey Arab soon became familiar to the locals. People would often stop to say hello to us and to ask how he is. He'd switch off his energy, rest a hind leg, and enjoy a few moments of being talked about, never looking for a fuss, but happy to chill out.

Neville is really nervous of large vehicles and as I could find out only so much about his past, I have to try and join the dots up myself. I've still not fathomed out his fear, and unfortunately for us we live in a farming and holiday location and at certain times of the year tractors and caravans are everywhere. Over the course of time Neville has grown less fearful, and will now try his upmost to stand his ground and let the larger vehicles go past. Gone mostly are the days thankfully that Neville would bolt past the vehicles and I'd have great difficulty in stopping him to try and turn him back to enable him to watch the vehicles driving away from us.

In his first year with us we were clocking up on average 100 miles a month out on the lanes. As he is barefoot and with the advice of my foot trimmer he wears hoof boots if we're on stony ground. This means we do not have any problem with him losing shoes if we are going through deep mud, and we've been on trails where water has come up to his knees and mud has covered his feet. He very rarely falters where I ask him to go he invariably goes. We've negotiated a track that we fondly call the Amazon trail that looked something out of the Tropics, full of mangroves with a stream running all along the centre of it, this highly strung horse worked his way along that trail, foot perfect. His only problem is open spaces, again as I do not know his history I have no idea why he goes into complete meltdown if I ride him into a field. He will change from a relaxed horse into a horse that simply wants to bolt, buck and spin. I don't think his ultimate aim is to get me off his back, it's almost like an explosion of energy, far too much energy for him to know how to handle.

The one time he has bucked me off in our open field, after galloping away, he suddenly realised I was no longer on his back, and turned round where I was getting up and brushing myself down, and simply trotted back to me.

Neville's ground work has always been suspect, to lead him simply from A to B from field to stable was interesting to say the least. He turned from this rather amenable 15.1hh horse to a snorting 18hh firebreathing Dragon who wants to hold his head up incredibly high almost lifting me up off the ground. He simply had no concept of good manners when being led, this would result in many a close shave with his teeth, as he would try and bite my arm almost in frustration of not knowing what was required of him.

If I tried to block his path if he went too far ahead of me, he would have no qualms in threatening with a flick of his front foot, it was almost in stallion fashion. I never really felt this was a major problem because to be quite honest leading him was not a large part of our daily life at home, He would always come to my call and at times when I needed to lead him he always seemed to comply with my requests.

Chapter 2
Neville's bit breaks.

The leading of Neville in extraordinary circumstances was tested on one occasion which led to a 5 mile walk home in-hand along a busy road with half a bridle tied round his face. When Neville came to me I knew the bit that he came with, was too long, and needed replacing immediately. Neville being Neville wasn't happy with just any bit, possibly due to the fact the one he had not fitting properly had on the few occasions that he'd been ridden given him a very uncomfortable mouth.

A good friend of mine lent me a sweet-iron bit for Neville to try. It was fairly old but one which fitted Neville to perfection and just as importantly Neville went very well in it. He started to listen to my hand aids and stopped fighting against this bit, but still on occasions would throw his head high up in the air, wanting to go faster than what I deemed a sensible speed.

On one particular occasion on an exceptionally hot Saturday morning, and with Rod accompanying us on his pushbike, it turned out to be a somewhat exhilarating ride.

We had been trotting along a fairly busy road and a few cyclists were coming towards us, I asked Neville to steady back from his ground covering trot, but Neville had other ideas, he just jutted his nose forward asking to go faster and in that precise moment it was when the old bit broke in half.

Suddenly I was riding a horse who already wanting to go faster, was now wearing a bridle with a broken bit, which was hitting him either side of his face on every stride. We were hurtling along this fairly busy road, with Neville now in canter with me holding onto reins that were attached to a flapping bridle with no bit.

All I could hear was myself saying "whoa Neville, whoa" I then without knowing if it would help or not, grabbed the neck strap which he wore whilst I was riding in case I needed a 'grab strap' and gave a pull back on it, keeping my legs long, and slightly tipping myself back.

This horse who was in full flow and panicking like mad beast, listened to my voice and my pulling on the next strap, and came back to a trot then to a walk and then finally to a halt. I quickly jumped off of him and looked back and there in the distance was Rod hurtling along on his pushbike who had seen it all happen ahead of him. I somehow managed to tie the bridle around Neville's face and all 3 of us had a long hot walk home. Bearing in mind Neville is not the easiest horse to lead, he showed me on this occasion that if the chips are down this horse will always try his best to behave. He seemed to fully enjoy the nudging and poking me in my back for the very long 5 mile walk home with me in full riding attire.

I learnt simple things like giving Neville a full bath was something Neville had not been used to. Any form of water on his face would cause Neville to lift his head high in the air completely out of my reach, I also learnt the last thing Neville will ever accept is cold water on him, he would almost fall to the floor, crunching his muscles tight and going into a spasm, so the simple trick is to always, no matter how hot the day is, to rinse Neville off in warm water.

Once he realised that the water was no longer freezing cold he was happy to have his face and body washed. I can remember that first magical moment with him having his head on my chest, me standing on the mounting block, both of us dripping wet where I had given him a full bath and put the sponge on top of his head to let the water run down his face, he looked almost as if he was smiling bless him.

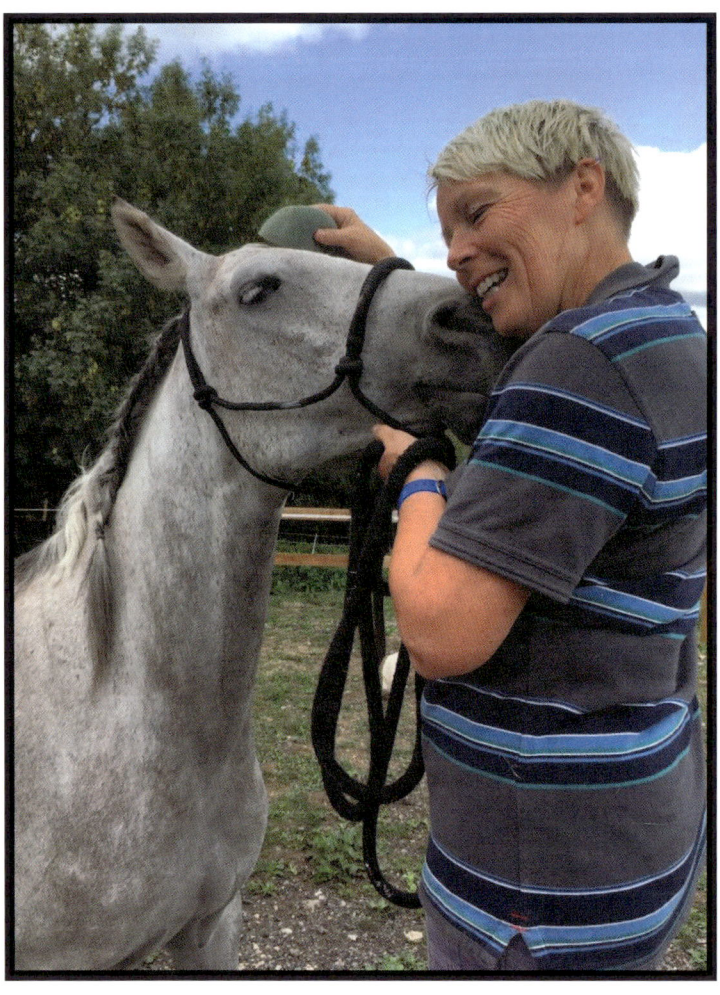

'Neville enjoying a face wash'

Now every morning Neville will have a warm wet flannel over his face, wiping out his nostrils and sleepy dust out of his eyes, it's just part of our daily routine which he is more than happy to accept.

Some of our rides out of the many miles covered, always hold a special place in my heart. One in particular was on a summer evening and Wilma accompanied Rod, Neville and myself along one of the two bridleways near us that was still usable at that time, but only if you had someone on foot to open the numerous gates. We walked around the edge of the first field and through the second gate, and if Neville has a track to follow he stays calm. We went through a further two fields and then along a chalk path. We came to a farm where we did a small circuit and then headed back in the same direction that we had come for Neville to have a canter along one of the grass tracks. When we got to the start of the spot that I'd chosen to canter Neville, Wilma who was a very well-behaved dog and was off the lead, looked at me as if asking if she too could come for a run. This was such a childhood dream to be galloping along the edge of a field with your faithful dog running alongside, to me it was simply the most magical of rides.

Chapter 3
Neville's accident

The majority of our hacking is solo, there are no other horses kept close to us therefore no one else to ride out with. On the very rare occasion I do ride out with another horse, it's because they have boxed over to us here. In the three years of owning Neville I have ridden out with others just five times. Neville's accident occurred on just the second time of riding out in company. He wasn't being silly, just a typical Arab, his head was a little bit up in the air and I don't think Neville was fully concentrating where he was putting his feet. On that particular day a friend of mine had called and asked if I'd like to go out for a quick ride with him, He boxed over two of his horses and brought along another person and the 3 of us went off for a ride. For all Neville's nervousness of large vehicles he is a courageous horse when going past busy farmyards, I was super proud of him leading the way out with two other horses that he had never met before. We were on our way home travelling down a country lane, there was a fair bit of gravel on the surface and we were all walking very steadily downhill. Neville's front feet slipped from underneath him and he went crashing down onto his knees. I only had time to say to him "Neville up, get up, up!" He scrambled to his feet and once he was upright I quickly jumped off. Blood was running down his near fore knee and we still had 40 minutes before we were home. I took a photo of his knee, called my vet, forwarded the photo and they said they'd be waiting for us when I got Neville home.

Neville was impossible to load onto any vehicle and it would've caused him more trauma for anyone to try and bring a trailer or van out, so the vet and I agreed it would be easier as I'm small and lightweight to simply get back on him and walk him steadily home. After a lengthy examination and portable x-rays it was discovered through sheer bad luck that through the cut on Neville's knee, gravel had gone into his tendon and had nicked the edge of it. It had not completely severed the tendon but what it did mean was lots of external and internal stitches under a local anaesthetic, and he had to have a cast put on, but would need it removed every 3 days for the wound cleaned and stitches to be examined.

Despite Neville's character he was a really good patient, the only time he was a tricky customer was when the vet came.

It wasn't too bad for the bandages to be changed in the early stages, but unfortunately the stitches did not hold and the healing process was an incredibly lengthy one. Granulation had to occur and it meant the heavy bandaging had to stay on for weeks on end, this did eventually cause a large sore to appear on the back of Neville's knee. It was at this stage of proceedings that Neville decided he would stand no more from the vet, it was deemed practical that I would become the vets assistant and under her watchful eye, I'd change the dressings. Neville and I became very close over the weeks he was on box rest, considering he was not even allowed to step foot outside his stable for me to muck him out, I think he kept incredibly calm.

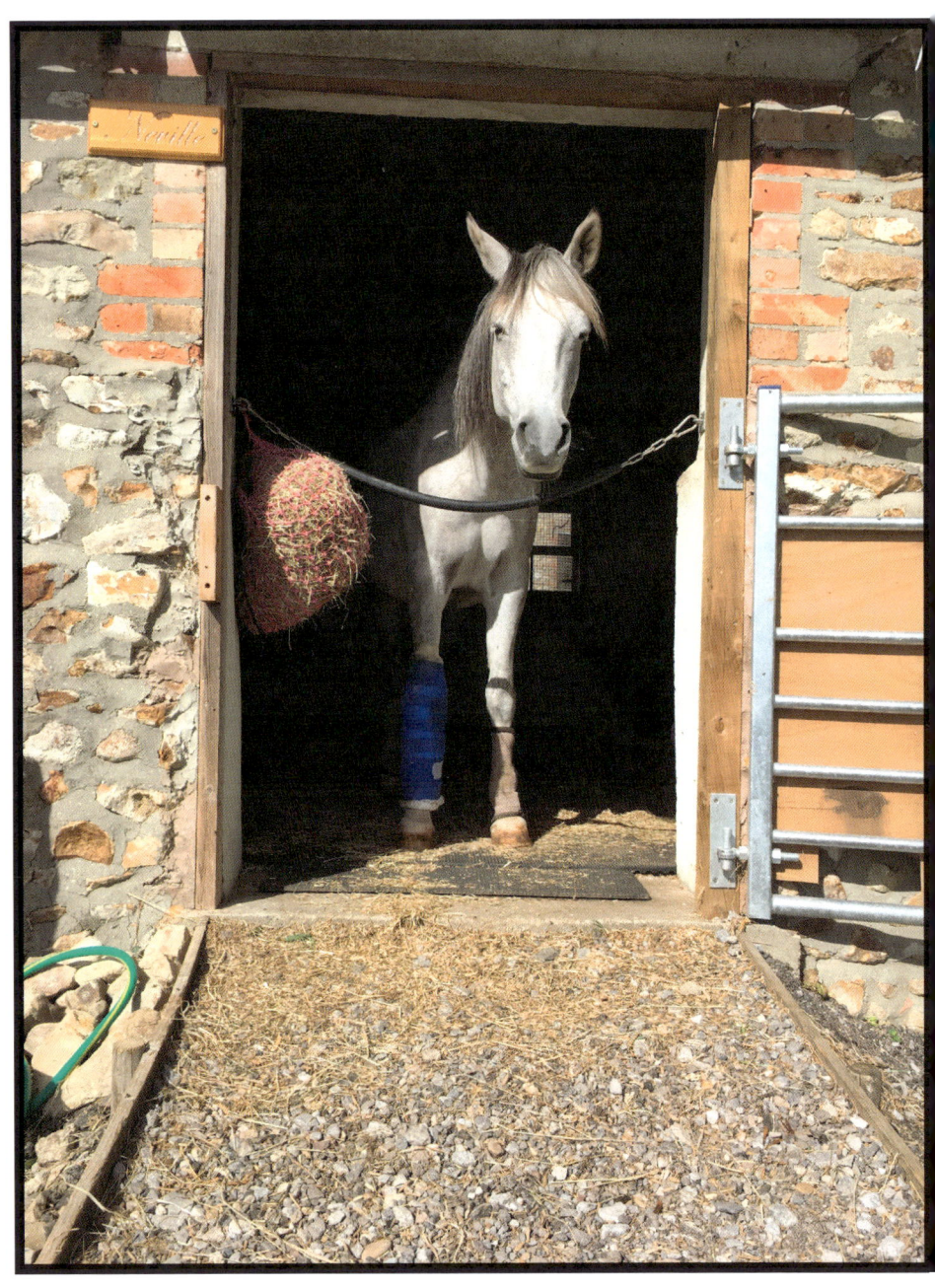

'Neville convalescing'

I put a strap across his stable door and I set up a deckchair and blankets on the ground immediately outside his stable where I would spend hours reading or laying in the sunshine with Wilma and blossom, all of us keeping Neville company. He was also the best groomed horse in the universe!

It came the day when the bandages were removed and Neville was given a 2 foot strip of his corral where he was allowed to stretch his legs just in this small space, it took a further 8 weeks of moving fencing across every two weeks to give him the full freedom of his fields. The joy of watching Neville squeal and buck feeling grass finally back under his feet was pure magic. Once he was back out, I lost my gentle pet and he turned back into the once again fully headstrong, stampeding, biting Arabian nutter!

I began the slow process of walking him out under saddle as he was more controllable ridden than being led, to regain his fitness and to ensure the muscle around his tendon became supportive again.

It was a nerve wracking time until further scans proved that the healing process had been fully successful. Once again I was back in the saddle doing what we both love, clocking up the miles.

It was soon after that time that I was put in touch with a natural horsemanship trainer, she is a highly skilled, knowledgeable lady who started to teach Neville and I the basics of natural Horsemanship groundwork. She is a force to be reckoned with and she and Neville soon had an understanding of just who was the boss! For the next six months I would have a regular monthly session, where both myself and Neville started to learnt a lot.

    Time went on and in those first 18 months of owning him, I knew that although he wasn't the easiest of horses, he was certainly mine. He was super loyal and he trusted no one else as much as he did me. I'd still have to be very respectful of his space, as he still had, and still has today, the tendency to tell you that you're overstepping his boundaries, always with his teeth. He'd allow me to touch him all over his face and clean minor wounds. His ears were still a no-go area if you needed to inspect them but it only took me just a few minutes now to tack him up rather than the hour to bridle him when he first came to us.

Chapter 4
The accident of all accidents

Neville and I were out on a sunny day, we were going to do one of our favourite rides, it's a 9 mile loop covering a fairly busy road but with lots of quiet country lanes. Looking back on this day, the first major hurdle should've been a warning of things to come. Something that neither of us had ever seen on our lanes nor expected to see, was coming very, very slowly towards us. It was an old traction engine, with full whistle as well! It was a glorious machine and obviously something the owner is incredibly proud of, but not something Neville and I were too impressed to meet on a narrow country lane. The noise was thunderous, imagine a huge metal roller thundering over tarmac with every rattle and creek accompanying every turn of the wheels. Not only that, but the driver seemed to think it was a good idea to blow the whistle to warn us that he was coming towards us.

That was one of my first times of riding Neville down one of the steepest hills I've ridden, whilst he was piaffing sideways and snorting like a true possessed dragon. It took 20 minutes for the traction engine to finally pass us where we had been tucked back in a farm track entrance, we then continued on our way for what I was obviously hoping to be a pleasant relaxed ride. We did the big loop on the countryside lanes in tranquil peace and quiet, it was wonderful. We were then back on the busy road to take us home. There seemed to be an abundance of delivery vans, cattle lorries, tractors and on top of it all, grass cutting work going on along a grass verge with strimmers. I paused in a gateway to allow 2 delivery lorries to go past us as well as a tractor coming towards us.

Neville was finding it all too much and did a little tap dance. When I looked down I noticed one of his hoof boots had come off. I went to dismount but stupidly hadn't realised Neville was completely zoned out of anything I was doing, and his adrenaline was sky high with all the traffic and the commotion of the grass cutting. With both my feet out the stirrups and with my right leg half over his back, he suddenly realised I was moving on his back and it was enough to send him into a blind panic. He bolted up the busy road, traffic in both directions, Neville zigzagged to the right and then to the left of the road narrowly avoiding an oncoming car, he was completely out of control and I was half on and half off. I tried to swing my right leg back over, almost got back into position but he then swung wildly to the left and I came off landing heavily on the road. Neville was on the left of me and jumped over me trying to avoid my body, but his hind hoof caught me on my temple. I was trying my utmost to not lose consciousness as I watched Neville galloping up the road away from me. I managed to lift myself up onto one of my elbows and shouted out his name, that horse who was already in total shock, slammed his brakes on, turned round and came back to me just as fast as he had run off. By the time Neville reached me, two people were standing over me where I'd dragged myself to the side of the road. No one had managed to get near Neville, all Neville wanted to do was to come and stand by me. I can remember fighting the nausea and above all wanting to sleep. I kept my hand on Neville's front foot and kept talking to him to reassure him and really to reassure myself.

Much against everyone's advice at the scene of the accident I managed to get back on Neville and ride him the 40 minutes home.

I do know that the traffic was still heavy but Neville never faulted and got me home, that's all I can remember about that ride home, but I can remember finally reaching the end of our track where I very carefully dismounted. I hung onto Neville and slowly made my way along our half mile track. Once nearly home I took my phone out of my pocket and thought it would be a good idea to call Rod to tell him about the accident, I also suspected due to the amount of pain I was in, I could well be looking at a trip to A&E.

It was quite close to lunchtime and I very rarely phone Rod as it is he that normally calls me to have our daily lunchtime chat.

The one day that I really needed to speak to him, it was a few minutes before his lunchtime, and Rod thought I had called him just for a slightly early lunch chat and hung up on me!!!

It took a further five minutes for Rod to call me during his allotted lunch break, by this time I was already at home……. I do like to remind him of his total negligence as often as possible!

He was totally horrified and quite beside himself, needless to say he immediately came home. He couldn't quite believe I'd somehow untacked Neville, gave him a sponge off & fed him a scoop of chaff, before I went indoors to survey the carnage of my face.

Rod took me to A&E where I spent the next nine hours being x-rayed and scanned. If we heard it once we heard it a million times, did I realise just how lucky I'd been, the fact that I was still alive and actually walking after a fall at that speed onto tarmac and to have a horse stand on my head?……. yes I did realise, and I truly thanked the powers that be, for keeping me alive that day.

A few days later I looked like a boxer after 10 bad rounds, but I was back in the saddle and bless him, Rod cycled with me to the scene of the accident to ensure both Neville and I weren't traumatised by it. One hairline crack to my elbow and one to my jaw along with a wobbly tooth, plus every bit of my body & right side of my face bruised, was the full extent of my injuries. I believe because I got back on and rode him home, Neville was never badly worried by that accident.

Just when you think all is good in the world, heartbreak hits. We lost Wilma, she was the absolute love of all our lives. Wilma was always with me whilst I mucked out, would trot along off leash when I rode out if Rod came too. She came everywhere with us when we were not at work, if anyone invited us overnight, they knew there was a little long nose guest too. She slept every single night for her 10 years wrapped around my feet under the duvet.

Quite simply we all went into decline and most noticeably was Blossom who had lost her big canine sister. They would play together, walk with me around the fields and they'd sleep curled up with one another.

We were bereft without a long nose in our pockets, so after a brief search Stanley-Pup was found. After a short time where Blossom hated him and Neville wanted to eat him, everything started to settle down once again in our lives.

'Dear Wilma & Blossom fast asleep together'

Chapter 5
Horace the Horsebox

After A few nightmare experiences with a beautiful trailer we had bought, resulting in a broken arm for me and severe trauma for Neville, Rod and I discussed the possibility of looking for a small secondhand horse van. Along came Horace the van. It's a side loading, rear facing van which I have to say after months of loading practice with Neville it's turned out to be an absolute godsend.

Before we even contemplated loading Neville in the van, we built an obstacle course in Neville's corral replicating the inside of the van with a ramp for him to step up onto. It was then that I discovered most of Neville's anxieties regarding loading him was him not fully comprehending his ability to turn on his haunches. When you watch horses running in the field and playing, they skip and turn every which way they wish to, but put them on a line and ask them to step over, it can often result in misunderstanding and resistance. After weeks of different obstacles requiring Neville to trust my voice he became very confident in not only squeezing into small spaces, but stepping forward, backwards and sideways. It was the true turning point of Neville loading confidently.

'Neville was finally loading calmly'

Neville became very proficient in his loading practice and the time came to load him up & take him to nearby woods and tracks. Our first adventure out in Horace, accompanied by Rod and young Stanley, was brilliant. Neville was a little tentative but soon got over his anxieties. It was our third trip out that really tested Neville's loading abilities. We'd parked in our usual place, off loaded him like a dream, tacked up & rode around the tracks and woodland for a couple of hours.

We came back to Horace, untacked Neville & loaded him foot perfect. We all jumped in the van, turned the key…. Nothing!

It was our worse nightmare, to be away from home with a horse that has a history of being incredibly difficult to load. We called the breakdown company who advised us, that as no one was in danger and we were off the road we weren't top priority and it may take a couple of hours to reach us. There was nothing for it but to off load Neville & take him for a walk in-hand back along the tracks to help keep him occupied. I saw Neville in a different light this day, he was the true dependable horse that I'd always dreamed of, Rod took Stanley and I held Neville on a longline and we simply ambled along the tracks. We stopped for Neville to nibble at grass and carried on walking in a totally relaxed manner. In fact what was a mini disaster would have been a really lovely chilled afternoon, if only we could guarantee that Neville would load.

We all mooched around for about an hour and came back to the van where I gave Neville a scoop of chaff whilst Rod decided to hop into Horace to see if by some miracle he could jiggle a few switches to get Horace to start again. Rod suddenly remembered he had one of his previous Christmas presents that we tend to buy one another and then sometimes forget we have, in the van's compartment. It was a multi tool kit which had the perfect tool to enable him to open the battery cover to the van. He discovered one of the leads were slightly loose, and once tightened he managed to start the van. We then had the joy of loading a horse that is prone to not loading, onto a van with the engine running. Neville was an absolute star, he loaded brilliantly, we shut the doors up and set off on our way home.

We called the breakdown company to let them know we no longer needed them and once home with Neville off loaded, we reflected on just how brilliant he'd been.

He had loaded, off loaded then re-loaded without one moment of hesitation. We had so many adventures planned, and were hoping for weekly trips out with Neville in the van, it was going to open a whole new world to us.

'Family outing in Horace the Horsevan'

Our lives as with everyone else's was about to change….

Chapter 6
Lockdown

Lockdown, we all now know what that means….. to us it meant with immediate effect we both started working from home. This was wonderful for Neville, Stanley and blossom, our way of life altered dramatically, we literally never left home unless it was to walk Stanley.

I stopped riding out on the lanes for six weeks as that was what was being broadcast, to avoid any activities that may put a strain on the already over loaded NHS. Lockdown has had a profound effect on Stanley, we had not realised he was becoming more and more institutionalised and was so used to having us at home 24 hours a day. It wasn't until after about four weeks into lockdown that we had to go out in Horace to collect Neville some food, we were going to leave Stanley at home, it was then we realised Stanley could no longer be left.

For the first four months of his life with us, he was left quite happily for my three days a week whilst I was at work, he had all of life's luxuries and comforts, with a big outdoor puppy playpen and lots of toys. Access was via a dog flap so he had all of indoors as well as outside space. I'd watch him from work on our various cameras, playing, eating and sleeping. Many a time one of us would forget to put the toilet roll up on the high shelf out of reach of Stanley, who would proceed to shred it causing a confetti covered home!

With Rod's Mum just next door, his little life seemed perfect. The moment lockdown hit, Stanley was not being left on his own without us.

My working hours were completely changed and as I was classed as a key worker I was to continue to work from home but instead of three days a week I was asked to work five days but on flexible working hours.

This is now a permanent arrangement and it's pretty fantastic for Neville, Stanley and Blossom. It does mean I can no longer go out for lengthy rides without a bit of planning around my work hours but it means I can have daily training sessions with Neville and Stanley without fail.

Although I'd obviously lost the ability to have my horse trainer come once a month during lockdown I started to read more and more and to watch various YouTube videos on natural horsemanship, this has since become a passion of mine.

My dear friend, the same friend who had lent me the horse bit all those months previous, suggested I entered a online horse challenge, a challenge run by a couple of wonderful ladies from a yard in Gloucestershire. For me this was the start of a whole new world and a whole new way of life with my relationship with Neville.

The Top Barn winter challenge 2021 was the turning point of mine and Neville's world.

Chapter 7
Introduction to the outside world.

I'm not a sociable person, there I've said it. Those that know me accept this simple fact. I'd like to think I'd do anything for anyone and I've been known to administer first aid to complete strangers, but invite us to a party and we'll politely decline. My Facebook page prior to top Barn held the grand total of 4 friends, and one of those was Rod.

One of the first requirements on the Top Barn online challenge was to introduce yourself along with your horse. I found pretty much straight away the Top Barn Facebook group was the escapism of my day to day work life that I used to find in books. Gone are the days of reading as I'm simply too busy with the 4 legs, but to share my day to day adventures of Neville and often Blossom and Stanley too, has given me immense enjoyment.

I won't give too much detail of the Top Barn winter challenge here, as it's very easy to find online, and anyone who reads and enjoys the sound of the challenge in these next few pages will hopefully be inspired by my tales and join up for the 2022 Winter challenge.

During December 2020 you could go on the TB12WC website and start downloading diaries, challenges, charts and timesheets to help plan and record your progress. You also had to choose what level you felt you and your horse would compete at, as well as choosing between 4 stages governed by how much time you could dedicate to valuable training or riding time with your horse.

The whole concept was invented by these fantastic ladies at Top Barn to give you focus during the 12 worse weeks of the year weather wise.

Due to Neville not being sensible to even lead in-hand, and riding in any form of large area was at best suspect, I decided I could dedicate 5 hours per week but at the basic level. As bad luck would have it, Neville nearly made the decision himself that meant we were about to withdraw before the official starting date of January 1st 2021. On December 2020 He was literally standing on only 3 legs.

The previous evening he'd had slight heat in his near fore hoof, but it was such a slight amount and as he was totally sound, I honestly didn't think there was too much to worry about. I knew the previous day he had come galloping up from his field and had stepped on a stone as he came in through the gateway, and I noticed he landed slightly awkwardly and took a couple of strides before he took weight back on it, but after that he looked fine. It was a bitterly cold evening when I went to call Neville up for his dinner, he nearly always came cantering up or at the very least at a very brisk walk, but this particular evening there was no sign of him.

I grabbed the torch and his head collar and went out in the dark to find him. He was the most pitiful sight to behold, there was Neville standing on the far side of the big field trying to take the weight off of his front foot, his head was lowered to the ground. The moment he saw me he started to chuff quietly, although he was wearing a rug he was freezing cold and shivering where he'd not been able to move around, and with the amount of pain he was in, he was also in shock. I had to leave him to run up to the house and grab my phone and let Rod know Neville was lame and in serious distress.

I felt terrible leaving Neville, he was calling to me as I sprinted back up to the bungalow. I got back to him as fast as I could and having already quickly called the vet who assured me he'd get to us as soon as possible. We started the slow painful journey up hill to his stable. I knew I had to encourage him to make that difficult walk as I needed to get him to the warmth and comfort of his stable. It took 45 minutes to get Neville up there, I was doing everything I could to get him to put one foot in front the other, he was in so much pain he grunted with every step. It was 10pm by the time we reached the stable and out vet was with us at 10.30pm.

Our vet had concerns that Neville may have broken his leg as there was no sign of any foot problem. He tested his whole foot with pinchers, but no reaction from Neville. After a lengthy 2 hour stint that wonderful patient vet found a very slight hint of a possible abscess. These can be incredibly painful for a horse, especially this type of abscess that had caused infection to travel up towards his knee. Neville was an absolute model patient with Stuart, who had never previously treated Neville as our regular vet was on maternity leave.

Neville was on 5 days, 24 hour box rest, not to be turned out until the pus had fully drained, this was to prevent any infection reaching the knee which would turn into a really serious issue. It meant I had to make a decision to drop out of the challenge completely or change from Silver to Bronze in the hope Neville would pull through and be back sound. I knew in the rules it stated you could have 1 week holiday and 1 week roll over, so in theory during the whole 12 week winter challenge you could just do 10 weeks but still ensuring you did the required amount of challenges and hours.

The Top Barn 12 Week Challenge had begun, not quite in the way I was hoping for, but Neville was up for the challenge as well as I was, even though he currently only had 3 good legs!

The Challenge is all about challenging yourself and your horse, to hopefully spend the winter months with a true focus, and to fulfil some goals. I chose my 10 challenges, all of which would push us both, but my first huge challenge was to treat the invalid!

Twice daily I had to remove the highly coloured Vetwrap dressings holding the Animalintex in place and 'tub' his foot in Epsom salts. This is where I quickly learnt to use a soft tub, rather than a normal rigid bucket with a handle, as on the first try, Neville ended up wearing the bucket with his leg through the handle, causing a major panic attack in the confined space of the stable, with me attempting to calm him down, avoid being kicked by Neville or clobbered by the flying bucket. I filled the tub half full of water as hot as you could put your hand in, to dissolve the Epsom salts, and asked Neville to stand his foot in it for at least 5 minutes. Morning and evening this took place, for the first few times I ended up with more over me or the stable floor, as needless to say Neville didn't have a clue what I was up to. I'm sure half the time he thinks I come up with these hair brained ideas just for fun. Once he realised it was actually quite soothing he was calm and such a good patient, it's times like this when Neville forgets his heritage and slips into behaving like the most gentle child's pony you could ever wish for.

The problems started when on day 3 Stuart the vet examined Neville and announced he still needed a further 2 days confined to barracks but I could start taking him for short walks in-hand so Neville could stretch his legs and have a nibble of grass. The vet had no idea what he was asking me to do. Neville when regularly ridden is still a force to be reckoned with when it comes to being led. I'm sure this stems from being held and punished in a previous life. He would go into panic then start fighting you. I'd learnt that I could lead him happily along our half mile track on the way home after a ride, as he associated that with pleasure, but in his brain anywhere else to be led, was going to cause him major problems. So armed with the thought that Neville needed some pleasurable time nibbling grass I put on a thick coat and riding hat to protect myself as best I could from teeth and hooves.

He was an angel…. I kid you not, for that first walk along the grass track he simply put his head down and munched on grass. He was in heaven, that was until his first of the 3 times a day, 30 minute sessions of being allowed out of his stable, had come to an end and I had to ask him to lift his head and point him in the direction of his stable. He quite literally exploded in temper, snapping in the air and waving his front feet in my direction… I took little comfort from the age old saying if they want to bite or kick you they will. It was all a huge bluff, threats to intimidate, but let me tell you it was seriously working. If it wasn't for the fact that he could be in possibly life threatening trouble if infection got into the bone, I'd never have risked life or limb leading that blooming great beast around and I would have put a field boot on him to keep the mud off his foot and turned him out.

So this continued for a further 3 days, 3 times a day….. did it get any easier, no not really, at times I felt like crying at the thought of fighting with him, but I did discover that singing out loud helped to not only calm my nerves but to pretend to Neville he wasn't scaring me.

The vet came back out, thoroughly checked Neville over who now was no longer in pain and was back to his usual character of being suspicious of everyone other than this crazy lady who adores him. Neville decided to thank Stuart by blasting him with one of his proper dragon snorts when the poor vet went to pat Neville on the neck to sign him off and to tell him he'd been a good boy. We both laughed as this was a good sign that Neville was back to his old self.

Chapter 8
The Top Barn 12 Week Winter Challenge

So one week into the 12 week Challenge and Neville was sound again and all he needed was a field boot on during the daytime to minimise risk of dirt getting into the small hole in his foot. I'd also completed the first of one of my chosen challenges, to be able to lead Neville in-hand. Admittedly it wasn't in quite the circumstances I was hoping for, but this intense week of handling him, being around him and leading him out 3 times a day, at least meant we had a bit more respect for one another, I lead, you follow and don't blooming bite me!

It was a very wet and incredibly cold start to the Top Barn 12 week winter challenge. Some days it was simply too foggy or icy to venture out onto the lanes. It seemed to permanently drizzle which made everywhere rather dreary.

Weather permitting I spent hours in the saddle clocking up the miles at every opportunity in between learning a lot of new groundwork skills. It's a fantastic community to be a part of, as you post your daily or weekly adventures, giving the highs and the lows. If you're having difficulty with one of your chosen challenges then all you need to do is ask for advice. Someone is always ready to give you ideas on how to achieve your goal.

I found it so interesting to see what others were up to, literally all stages of horse skills were here on the group. Some had unbroken youngsters which were obviously non ridden, others had horses too small to be ridden, others had horses far more experienced than my Lad who was still learning basic manners. What we all had in common though was the same goal, to get through the winter giving ourselves and our horses challenges to see us through the bleak months and a sense of camaraderie.

During the entirety of the 12 weeks I was required to work with Neville 3 hours a week, and this was not to include the usual daily grooming, mucking out or rug changing, but must be training or riding. I hit it with an absolute passion and each week I'd more than double the required hours. My best week on the hours was on week 8 where I worked with Neville 11.5 hours, this was whilst working at least 5 hours a day, Monday to Friday at my grown up desk job.

I'd be up at 5.45am to start the day, it was hard work but so incredibly rewarding.

One of my other challenges was the goal of riding out every week no matter what the weather for a minimum of 5 miles. This is obviously incredibly easy in the summer months, not so easy when you have ice on the roads for days on end. We managed by the end of the challenge well over 120 miles.

I also chose a challenge where Neville had to complete a figure 8 whilst at liberty, so no rope attached, only listening to your voice and being guided by your hand signals. Neville had never tried anything like this before, we were absolute newbies at this fancy groundwork malarky, purely because in the 6 months of monthly lessons previous to lockdown, we'd been concentrating on working with Neville's confidence issues.

Neville despite his high energy and often aggressive attitude if he doesn't understand something and feels you're not explaining it correctly, decided Liberty work was his forte, but only in the safety of his corral.

To take him beyond his comfort zone would result in him having a major melt down, where he'd try and bite or kick you, he was not going to make anything easy.

He understood the concept of walking a circle around me but it took massive concentration on his behalf to listen carefully, to halt when asked, to turn this way or that way, to step towards me or away from me.

The figure of 8 seemed such a good idea when I first chose it, but my goodness it took weeks of breaking it down, for him to remain calm enough to complete just half the figure 8, we had a long way to go.

My final chosen challenge was to jump Neville in the roundpen over a 'proper' jump. Neville when being loose schooled over a pole flat on the ground would jump it as if it was a 2' bar and to send him over a jump of just 18" would cause him to jump as high as if he was clearing a 5 bar gate…. what on earth was I thinking of!

There was, halfway through the 12 weeks a separate competition called the Mid challenge, this was only open to premium paid up members of the 12 week challenge which I was one of. You were set a task of performing a video of you and your horse, in-hand, ridden or at liberty of going 'over' something, 'under' something, 'around' something, 'pick up' an object and to step back 3 paces.

'Neville's first look at the arch, and he really wasn't sure!'

Neville and I worked hard on preparations for this. Rod helped me make an arch and 3 elevated trotting poles for Neville to step over. I wrapped all the wooden poles in brightly coloured gaffer tape to help keep them waterproof but mainly just to make them look pretty! I laid a tarpaulin held on the ground by a wooden pole either side for Neville to walk along.

Seeing as Rod and I had made all these props ourselves and Neville never trying anything like this in his life before, we didn't disgrace ourselves. Neville was fast gaining himself a little fan club on our Top Barn Facebook group for his sheer Arabian attitude to everything.

His head tossing flamboyance to life and plus not always hiding the fact that he can be the most anxious of horses, seemed to bring out the maternal instincts in a lot of the group, who came to know his background but could honestly see how hard he was trying to be brave and give everything a go.

'We worked each day on the various obstacles'

It was an eye opening to see just what Neville could be capable of, no more dwelling on his past, thinking of the 'might have beens' and the 'what if's' but looking now to what we could achieve if we learnt to fully trust one an another.

'Neville concentrating stepping over raised poles'

I had to stop thinking of Neville as damaged goods, and really start to work out ways of communicating with him to try and prevent the trigger switches that caused his aggressive behaviour.

The majority of his behaviour stems obviously from his past and continuous mistrust of all humans, but also from being incredibly clever and not forgiving idiots like me for not explaining things correctly.

If I wanted him to step away from me I've since learnt that all I have to do is raise my hand towards either his face if I wish his head to move away from me, or to place my hand towards his bottom for him to move his haunches away from me.

This was once of course he began to trust me enough to realise a raised hand was not to punish him. Horses aren't born to understand humans and our hand signals, but with repetitive daily sessions Neville soon started to forgive all my clumsy antics and to start to working with me.

Neville seems to enjoy nothing better than a 10 minute early morning training session in the safety of his stable or corral, where it would be just me and him and a pocket of treats, with me asking him to step this way, or that way, or to spin all the way round. Neville also seems to get immense enjoyment from simply standing on his platform showing off, and he'll often be seen to be doing his own thing completely unaided whilst Rod and I are watching him from the kitchen window.

We still had a long way to go in being able to walk calmly side-by-side whilst Neville was in-hand, but what I did achieve during the 12 weeks was a far better understanding in my ability to communicate with Neville and to put a lot more faith in my own judgement. The day I'd planned to film jumping my flying desert horse, turned out to be a bit of a wet and windy one. Only having a set period of time naturally means you end up playing mind-games with yourself, if I leave the filming to another day it could be raining harder, would I then be unable to fulfil this particular challenge and simply run out of time?

'Neville choosing to stand on his platform, what a stunner!'

So I carried on with the jumping challenge, and we did it! Neville's first jump with me on his back over the blocks and poles Rod had bought me for my birthday at the beginning of winter. Neville's habit of launching into bucks when cantering in open spaces and the roundpen has meant I've been somewhat cautious with what I do with him, but somewhere along our journey we were getting there. That day I felt such elation in taking this 15.1hh horse over a tiny 2' cross pole that my joy and pride in him was indescribable. Over the years I've jumped 3' cross country courses and competed regularly in show jumping, but I have to say I felt every bit as proud for this achievement as I did in those younger competitive days.

'Neville approaching the small cross pole'

We still had the last challenge of the figure 8 at liberty to complete within the 12 week period, and we were fast running out of time, we wouldn't lose anything other than the completion of a task set by yourself, but it was a matter of pride. I worked a little morning and evening on trying to crack the missing link in Neville understanding with what I was looking for in that figure 8. He'd walk the first half then simply stop. I still needed to fit in my daily 5 hours grown-up job, as well as ensuring Stanley and Blossom didn't miss out on any attention. I also needed to maintain the riding hours to keep Neville up to his winter fitness. I was feeling a bit frustrated when I decided to forget the first half of the 8, and simply concentrate on the right hand loop, it only went and worked! Neville had been getting anxious about approaching me from a different side, so after showing him that it's ok to do that, his figure of 8 at liberty is now one of his 'go-to' patterns if he feels like a liberty session.

That completed the 3 challenges I'd set for us, as well as completing the Top Barn 12 week winter challenge. We'd clocked up just over 120 miles during a tough winter and 92 hours of training. There were many adventures encountered on those miles and hours, and we had well and truly earned our rosette along with Rod who'd helped and supported me in anything I asked. In fact Rod was bought his very own rosette as a thank you for his commitment to us completing this awesome challenge.

'My amazing husband who spent hours keeping me sane'

The Top Barn 12 week winter challenge was over, we had not only completed it, we'd smashed the Bronze hours and had also completed the Silver requirements. No one could possibly have been prouder of their great grey nutter.

'The eureka moment when Neville completed the figure 8'

It had been a hard 12 weeks, but I never regretted one minute of it and I can't wait for the Top Barn 12 Week Winter Challenge of 2022. Neville and I will be there again giving it our best shot.

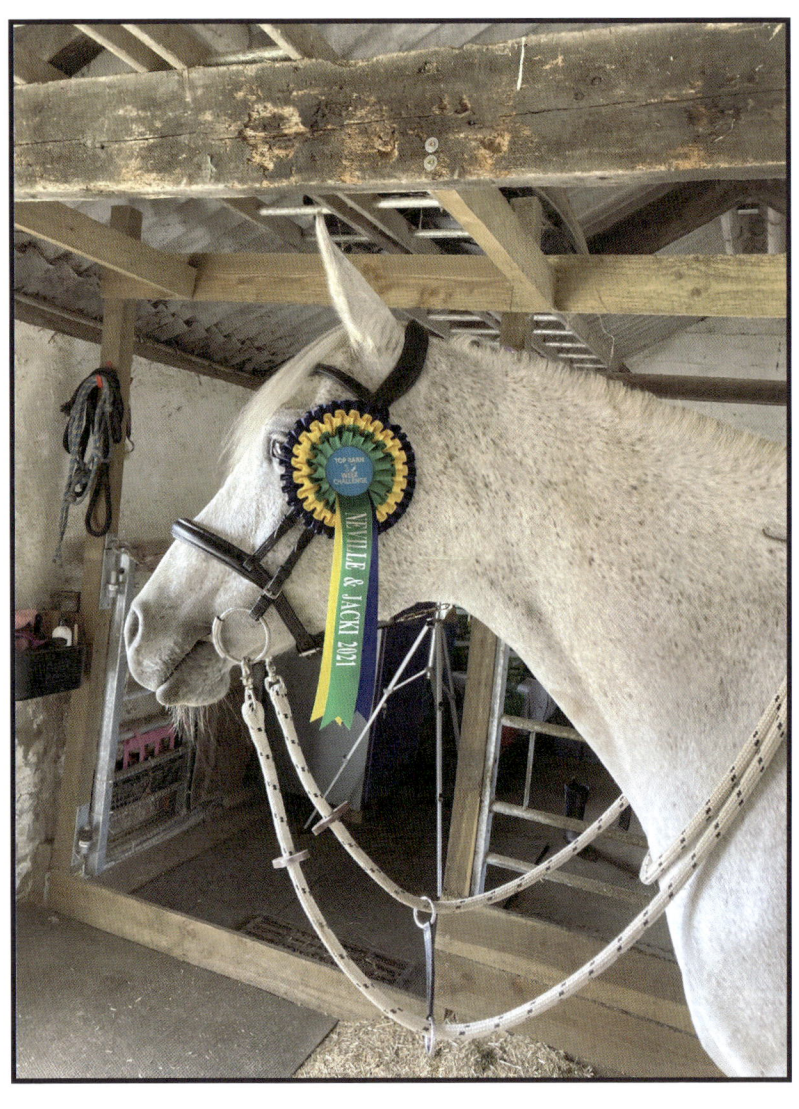

'Neville wearing his beautiful well earned first ever rosette'

Chapter 8
Neville's first showing classes

I think what The Winter Challenge did for Neville and myself was to make us realise there was more to life than simply clocking up the miles out on the lanes. We had met a community of like-minded people who simply enjoyed doing different things with their horses, albeit online.

What lockdown has done for me was to make me look outside the box, Neville would never have enjoyed actually attending shows but joining an online community meant I can practice at home and actually record any of the show classes here as well. In May we were advised that they were organising shows and dressage competitions throughout a few of the summer weeks. Classes were put up on the HUB website and I sat and pondered over which classes I thought Neville and I could possibly enter.

I had only just started recently riding Neville in the roundpen and he could still be somewhat interesting at times, he was known to buck and gallop around as if the very Devil was on his tail, but after some very helpful advice from a lady called Cheryl who has now become a very dear friend, I put into practice all that she suggested and I could finally see the results. Neville was becoming more in tune with me and less anxious when being ridden in the roundpen but his in-hand work was still too unpredictable to be deemed safe at this time for attempting any trotting along next to me.

I decided to enter Neville in a class which showed off his trot which I would do out in our little yard, where he'd been regularly trotted in-hand for vet inspections during his tendon injury to his knee.

I'd also entered a ridden class where we both had to look smart, and finally a class which was called 'The horse the judge would most like to take home'. I decided Neville could do what he loves, some liberty work incorporating his platform. The show classes where great fun to practice, and I thoroughly enjoyed the actual filming of them. Although I felt very nervous filming us, being at home also meant if it didn't go well on that first take, you could always have another try.

I had a whole month to try and prepare Neville to see if I could get him to walk and trot in hand alongside me in the roundpen, I was practising this on a regular basis, but when the final day came for filming I still decided not to risk unsettling him and to stick to my original plan of trotting him up in hand out in the yard.

Never having entered Neville in anything like this before, I was absolutely amazed and thrilled that Neville was placed third in the class for The horse the judge would most like to take home. Neville had performed this beautifully and incredibly enthusiastically which totally sums up his whole character.

'Neville standing proudly on his platform in his first show'

'Neville and I in the class 'Smartest pair'

No one could've been prouder than I was of my reject, project horse that's slowly becoming so much more than I'd ever dreamt of.

He'll never be an easy horse, possibly he'll never be the safest, but what Neville will always be is my horse with true grit, my horse with spirit.

He has finally chosen to trust me, it's taken over three years to get to where we're at today, I know we'll still have our discussions, but what I also know is we're going to have a lot more adventures in the future.

'Neville after enjoying a bath'

****

Since the completion of this story, Neville and I went on to compete in the 'Top Barn Summer Challenge' where you had 8 weeks to complete four stages of a gruelling challenge.

Neville and I were one of the few to complete all four stages, he did this with his usual courage, humour and above all, true Arabian grit and determination.

****

'Neville calmly wearing all 4 of his rosettes

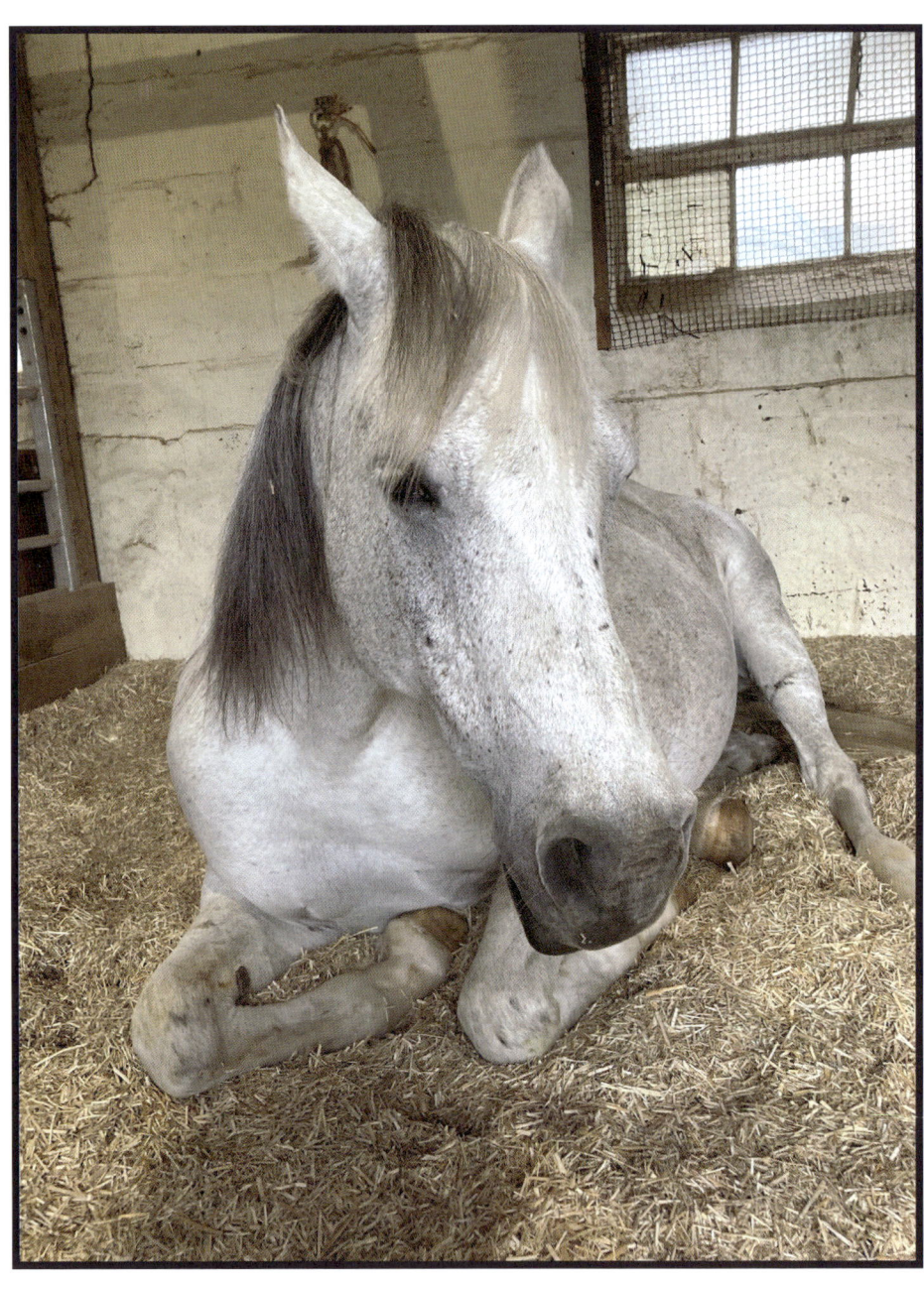

'Neville is my forever horse'

Huge thanks to Zoe and Rhian who run Top Barn and find the time to organise all the wonderful online completions throughout the year.

Most of all, heartfelt thanks to my wonderful Husband who never fails to have faith in me.

Printed in Great Britain
by Amazon